BARRON'S

Engelbert Kötter

My # Gerbil
and Me

With: Ehrenfried Ehrenstein
Photographs: Christine Steimer
Illustrations: Renate Holzner

Stories: Gabriele Linke-Grün

Contents

Building Trust from the Start

love it

Gerbil Adventures

Fun and Games with Gerbils

have fun

Active and Happy in Old Age

old & happy

Golden

Nibbling and gnawing, climbing and hiding, scampering around or taking a sand bath, nuzzling each other—these are the activities gerbils like best. Gerbils enjoy a wide variety of healthy foods, along with an occasional plump sunflower seed, mealworm, or nut as a special treat. If you give your gerbils proper care, they will respond with remarkable trust.

Rules
for Proper Care

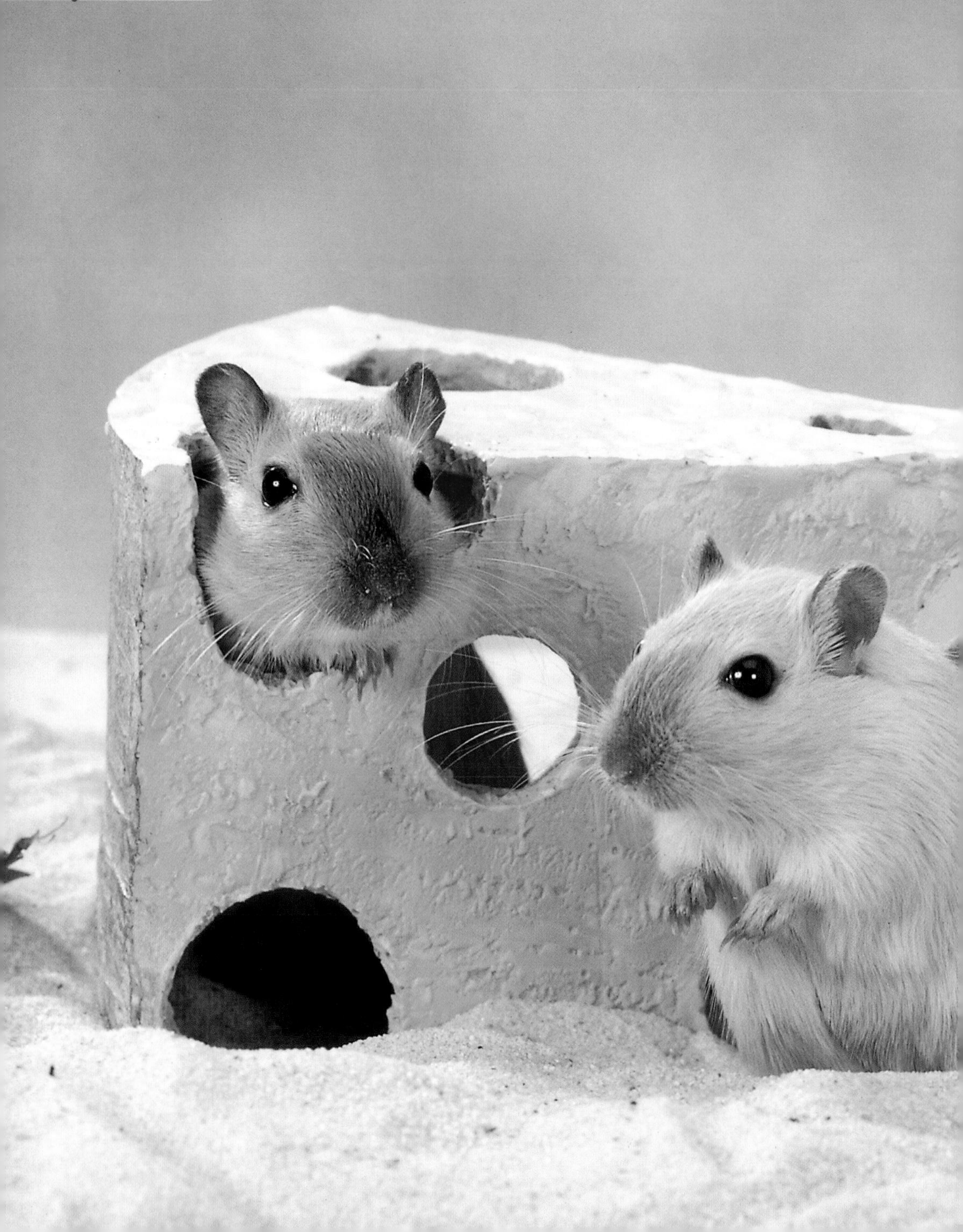

The 10 Golden Rules for Equipment

1 A multilevel cage, as spacious as possible, is best for gerbils. For two gerbils, the minimum size is 12 × 22 inches (30 × 55 cm).

2 A large aquarium or terrarium can also provide suitable shelter.

3 If you are handy with tools, you might want to link several cages or aquariums to create a multi-room enclosure.

4 Line the cage with commercial bedding or clean sand. Also provide soft nesting materials (such as straw or paper towels).

5 Supply plenty of small pieces of wood, branches from suitable trees, and cardboard boxes for your gerbils to gnaw on.

6 These energetic little rodents enjoy running in a metal exercise wheel.

7 Climbing structures made of stones, boards, or slabs of bark offer hiding places and opportunities for play.

8 A cardboard tube is useful for transporting your gerbils back into their cage.

9 Install a drip-free water dispenser that hangs from the side of the cage.

10 A shallow porcelain dish filled with bird sand makes an inviting sand bath for gerbils.

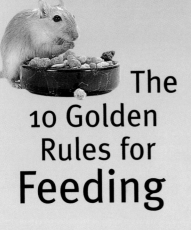

The 10 Golden Rules for Feeding

1. Gerbils prefer a varied diet of healthy foods.

2. For their basic food, offer your gerbils a grain mixture, with oatmeal, sugar-free granola, hamster feed, or even a little birdseed.

3. A piece of hard cracker now and then makes a tasty treat.

4. Offer small amounts of suitable vegetables: carrots, endive, chicory, cucumbers, cooked potatoes.

5. Never feed gerbils sorrel, raw beans, or moldy potatoes.

6. Gerbils love to munch on many different kinds of fruit.

7. Nontoxic twigs (for example, from birch, beech, hazel, and fruit trees) also satisfy a gerbil's need to gnaw.

8. Now and then, offer protein in the form of a few mealworms, chopped hard-boiled egg, or yogurt. Mother and baby gerbils, in particular, crave animal protein.

9. Sunflower seeds, pumpkin seeds, and nuts are delicacies to be given sparingly.

10. Change the drinking water supply at least once a week.

take care

The 10 Golden Rules for Care

1 A gerbil needs the company of at least one other gerbil in order to thrive.

2 Place the cage in a dry, well-lit location that is protected from cold, drafts, and noise.

3 Clean the cage thoroughly at least once a month.

4 Remove droppings and soiled bedding regularly.

5 Be sure your gerbils always have fresh twigs, wood, or cardboard to gnaw on.

6 Any leftover fresh food must be taken from the cage the next day.

7 You can place the grain mixture right on the sand or other cage bedding.

8 Gerbils need frequent opportunities to exercise outside their cage in a gerbil-proof room.

9 Gerbils that are roaming free may return to their cage on their own, if they can easily do so. If you need to catch them, it's best to use a cardboard tube so they won't learn to fear your hand.

10 Never grab or hoist a gerbil by the tail—it will break off very easily.

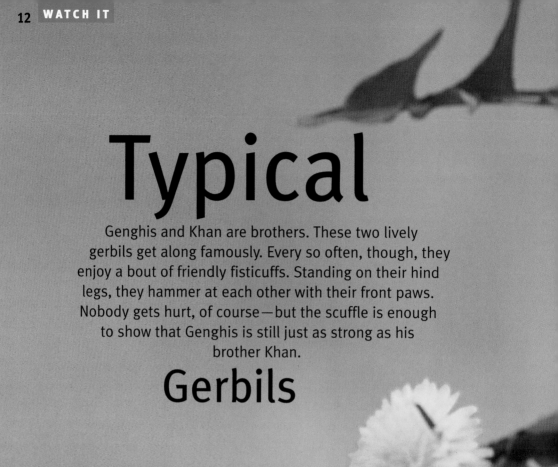

Typical

Genghis and Khan are brothers. These two lively gerbils get along famously. Every so often, though, they enjoy a bout of friendly fisticuffs. Standing on their hind legs, they hammer at each other with their front paws. Nobody gets hurt, of course—but the scuffle is enough to show that Genghis is still just as strong as his brother Khan.

Gerbils

At Home on the Steppes

The cute, furry rodents known as Mongolian gerbils have become popular pets only in recent decades, but their popularity is more than justified. Their native habitat is the steppes—the semiarid, grass-covered plains of Mongolia, in east-central Asia. There, they dig extensive burrows for shelter from the winter cold and summer heat, preferably in areas where shrubs offer cover when they emerge. Taking luxurious sand baths, burrowing and scraping in the ground, and darting from one protected spot to another are typical behaviors of gerbils in the wild. Pet gerbils exhibit the same interesting habits. Their dietary needs likewise resemble those of their wild relatives. Grain forms the bulk of the diet, but gerbils also relish juicy green plants, fruit, and insects from which they obtain moisture. Gerbils seldom drink water—a plus for the pet owner, because they excrete little urine.

Gerbils Live in Clans

In the wild, families of gerbils form colonies. In each burrow, the parents live with as many as two litters at a time, until the older youngsters mature and form clans of their own. Gerbils recognize clan members by their odor. By mutual grooming, they mark each other with saliva that carries a distinctive scent—a signal that says, "This gerbil is one of us."

Their native habitat, the steppes of Mongolia, still influences the ways of gerbils. They love to burrow and take sand baths.

Genghis and Khan

As I studied the lively clan of gerbils before me, two brothers caught my eye right away. No question—these were the gerbils for me. Furthermore, I knew right away what I would name them. In honor of their ancestral homeland, the steppes of Mongolia, I called the bolder brother Genghis and the more cautious little fellow Khan. Their distinguished namesake was Genghis Khan, the mighty conqueror who founded the Mongol Empire. I was proud of the comfortable dwelling that awaited my new pets. The spacious cage held roots for the nimble rodents to climb and hide among, a generous pit for sand baths, soft straw for bedding, and all sorts of things to gnaw on. I fully expected that Genghis and Khan would set right to work to con- struct a cozy sleeping nest—but Genghis had something else in mind. First of all, he wanted to test the strength of the cage. Standing up tall and using his tail for extra stability, he braced his front paws firmly against the cage door. Sure enough, the door sprang open, and Genghis lost no time in scooting out into the room. Meanwhile, Khan crouched under a root in the cage, waiting to see whether the adventure would go well. Indeed, it went well for Genghis—but it taught me a lesson. I had left my mystery novel on the floor with a bookmark to hold my place. Quick as a wink, Genghis found the book and seized the last several pages in his paws. Before I could stop him, the little marauder had torn them to shreds with his sharp teeth. Alas, it would be several days before I could purchase another copy and find out whether the butler had committed the crime!

Solitude Is Boring

Because gerbils are highly social creatures, it's best to keep at least two. However, they need not necessarily be a pair; two gerbils of the same sex can also live in harmony. Experience shows that siblings get along best. Two brothers are particularly compatible. As females mature, the likelihood of scuffles between them increases.

Gerbils feel secure only when they share a nest with other gerbils. Indeed, they may curl up in a pile as many as three layers deep! While some sleep or doze, others are busy grooming them. The social behavior of gerbils is not limited to the sleeping nest. Even when they are roaming free, gerbils will sniff at each other whenever they meet. In the wild, gerbils identify others of their own clan by their odor. Two gerbils of equal strength sometimes pummel each other in a friendly tussle. But woe to any intruder—these otherwise quite affable creatures will fight fiercely to repel a gerbil from outside the clan.

For the most part, however, the daily life of gerbils features companionship, mutual grooming, and lively, playful activity.

What Gerbils Are Like

→ Gerbils are furry, ratlike rodents that belong to the family Cricetidae. Mongolian gerbils make excellent pets.

→ Their homeland extends from southern Mongolia to northeastern China.

→ In the wild, groups of gerbils live in colonies.

→ These rodents eat primarily grains and seeds.

→ Fruit and vegetables, as well as mealworms and other insects, add variety to a gerbil's diet.

→ Gerbils need plenty of exercise and materials to gnaw on if they are to thrive.

→ The life expectancy of pet gerbils is three to four years, about two years longer than in their natural surroundings.

→ Domesticated gerbils have been bred with many attractive color markings.

→ Pet gerbils will become extremely trusting, but rarely completely tame to the touch.

→ Gerbils are active both day and night, with a sleep-and-wake cycle of two to four hours.

The size of a gerbil colony should not exceed 10 to 15 animals. Otherwise, quarrels are more frequent and more likely to lead to serious strife.

From Stranger to Friend

It's best to start with two or more gerbils that have already formed a group. A solitary gerbil needs a companion, but introducing the newcomer can present problems. Keep in mind that gerbils don't welcome other gerbils whose smell is strange to them.

Young gerbils, six to eight weeks old, can usually be placed together without difficulty. Older animals need very careful handling while they get to know each other. The following method has proved successful: Divide a small cage (or aquarium) in half with a strong piece of wire mesh. Be sure not to leave any holes the little beasts could sneak through! Place one gerbil in each half of the cage with an ample supply of bedding. For a few days, switch the position of the two gerbils several times a day. Each time, put a handful of bedding from each side into the opposite side of the cage. This process gradually blends the odors of the two gerbils until they share a common odor that both of them recognize and accept. After about a week, try putting the two gerbils together in a small manageable area outside the cage. Watch for scuffles; if they escalate or persist, separate the animals immediately and resume the switching process.

To pick up a gerbil without alarming it, use both hands and an open palm.

TIP from the BREEDER

Gerbils have been bred with many attractive color markings. However, those who want to breed gerbils may have difficulty finding parents with the newer markings. Fortunately, the Internet offers a number of sites where gerbil fanciers can communicate and even exchange breeding animals.

If the encounter is peaceful, place the two gerbils together in the normal large cage, along with the blended bedding from the divided cage. Stay vigilant until you're sure the two will live in harmony.

Is Breeding a Goal?

The many enjoyable experiences of owning gerbils include watching the birth and development of baby gerbils. However, the process of breeding gerbils requires careful planning. Are you prepared to care for the large family that will result? Keep in mind that a female gerbil can mate and become pregnant again on the same day that she gives birth to a litter. If you intend to give away the youngsters, you must have willing takers. Don't count on pet stores to accept an unlimited number of half-grown gerbils.

If the gerbils' cage becomes too crowded as the offspring mature, you can connect several cages (or terrariums or aquariums) with drain pipes, forming tunnels that allow some of the gerbils to establish a new nest in another area.

If you decide to stop breeding your gerbils, divide the group into separate cages. Place the father with two young males and the mother with two young females. This strategy takes into consideration that the parents, who are usually quite a bit older, have a shorter life expectancy. If the older gerbil dies, the two young siblings will still have each other for company. If you want to separate the parents from their offspring as a pair but intend to stop breeding them, consult a veterinarian about having one or both of them neutered.

Raising Young Gerbils

Gerbils are monogamous. It's best to choose a breeding pair of the same age, so that they can stay together for as long as possible. The mating ritual often lasts for half a day. Then you will have to wait 23 to 26 days until the baby gerbils are born. If the mother gerbil is already suckling another litter during the pregnancy, the gestation period can last twice as long.

The pregnant female becomes increasingly slow and ponderous as time goes on. She waits until the very last minute to prepare the nest for birthing. Shortly before the babies are born, she banishes all the other family members from the nest. They must build and move into a new nest.

The mother and the father gerbil care for their young together. If the mother leaves the nest, the father will often slip in to keep the hairless newborns warm. Also, the mother may cover them with nesting material. This means that during their first days of life you are more likely to hear the little ones squeaking than to see them. After four days, the baby gerbils start to sprout the first tips of fur; after about three weeks, they open their eyes. Around this time, they begin to scramble from the nest—more work for the mother, who seizes each small adventurer by the scruff of the neck and carries it back to safety. At about five weeks old, the gerbils are independent. But they do not become sexually mature for another two weeks.

→ For happy gerbils: Bringing up baby gerbils is hard work for the parents, especially the mother. Support the female during pregnancy and lactation with extra servings of high-protein food. Good choices are plain yogurt or, as a special treat, mealworms (sold in pet stores).

Another reminder: For the first two weeks after the babies are born, make every effort to leave the little family in peace and quiet. Because you won't want to disturb the nest during the period when the babies are most vulnerable, give the cage a thorough cleaning before they arrive. The next cleaning will be due when the youngsters are about six weeks old. For their own safety, the little ones should stay in the cage until then.

A gerbil must have the companionship of another gerbil in order to thrive.

Khan Takes a Detour

From the minute they wake up, gerbils are ready
for action. Genghis and Khan are no exception.
For this reason, even though they live in a spacious multilevel enclosure, I give them plenty of
opportunities to roam free around the room. When
the two little fellows have had their fill of exploration
and adventure, they usually go back into their comfortable
cage of their own accord. One evening, however, events
took a different turn. Genghis had returned to the cage
at least an hour before and was quietly dozing, but
Khan was nowhere in sight. Systematically, I searched
every corner of the room, but found no trace of the
small adventurer. At last, I gave up the search. "He'll
find his way to the food dish when he gets hungry," I
thought to myself, and I closed the door of the room
and went to bed. But when I checked the cage in the
morning, I saw only Genghis, still curled up and sound
asleep in his little nest. Again I made a thorough
search of the room—again, without success. Worried, I
began my morning chores. The first task was to empty
the wastepaper baskets, because today was recycling
day. Somewhat distractedly, I hoisted the nearest basket.
Suddenly, I heard a suspicious
rustling sound. Looking inside, I
saw Khan valiantly struggling to
the surface of the heap of papers.
The lost wanderer was found! Of
course, it should have occurred to
me to look in the wastepaper
basket—a gerbil can
easily manage to jump
from the floor into such an
inviting receptacle. It seemed,
however, that jumping out again
was another matter for my little Khan.

The Senses

Vision: Gerbils see objects at a distance better than those close by. Their depth perception is not particularly good, because their eyes' individual fields of vision just barely overlap. However, if a gerbil needs to estimate a distance more closely, for example in order to jump over a small ditch, it uses a little trick: Standing up on its hind legs, it nods its head up and down. Apparently a nearby object moves more in the gerbil's field of vision than a distant object—a phenomenon you can try for yourself! Because a gerbil's dark shoe-button eyes protrude so far, it can see in almost all directions at once. This allows the gerbil to detect an enemy, such as a hawk in the sky, in time to take shelter.

→ For happy gerbils: Never try to pick up a gerbil from above. The gerbil would feel as if a bird of prey had seized it and would be terror-stricken. Any trust you had already won would vanish, and you would have a very hard time regaining your pet's confidence.

Hearing: While the range of human hearing extends only to about 20,000 hertz, gerbils can also hear sounds at higher frequencies. However, a gerbil's hearing varies in sensitivity at different frequencies. Young gerbils hear best at 15,000 hertz, older ones at 4,000 hertz. Whether young or old, gerbils can hear frequencies far into the ultrasound range. We know that young gerbils call to their mother in voices so high-pitched as to be inaudible to others.

On their first outing into the wide world, these young gerbils display both curiosity and caution.

→ For happy gerbils: Be sure to locate their cage in a quiet place. Shrill music, slamming doors, and other loud noises make your small friends tense and fearful.

Smell: A gerbil's keen sense of smell plays a crucial part in its orientation to the world. If our noses were as sensitive as a gerbil's, we would be able to smell our food much better than we do. Even more important, we would be able to tell with our eyes closed whether a person were a relative or a stranger. And our world wouldn't need fences, for we, like gerbils, could sense where our territory ended and a foreign territory began.

→ For happy gerbils: Your pets recognize you by your distinctive personal odor. Take care that your hands don't smell of perfume, lotion, or other strong aromas when you handle your gerbils.

Touch: Gerbils use their long whiskers to determine whether a hole is large enough to creep through, as well as to orient themselves, especially in the dark. Even in daylight, the whiskers provide useful information, because gerbils don't see nearby objects well. When danger threatens, gerbils drum their hind legs on the ground, creating vibrations that send a warning to other gerbils. A gerbil's front paws are also very sensitive.

A job well done! Now that all the straw has been reduced to shreds, it's time for the gerbils to tidy up and groom their coats.

→ For happy gerbils: Set the cage on a stable foundation in a place that is not exposed to vibrations.

Typical Behaviors

Fighting: When two gerbils meet, they sniff each other thoroughly to identify fellow clan members. Strangers will be bitten and driven away. Another form of tussling occurs among clan members: Now and then, the gerbils pummel each other with their front paws in a sort of boxing match. Young gerbils, in particular, test their strength in these playful bouts. The one that loses will lay its head on the ground below that of the winner to demonstrate submission.

Dashing about: Gerbils often roam about their cage, from one corner to another, or dash at top speed across the cage. For this reason, the cage should be as spacious as possible. Of course, gerbils enjoy such sprints even more when they have the run of the room outside the cage.

Darting out from hiding: Gerbils typically dart out from a hiding place, then turn and scoot back in again. In the wild, mastering this flight behavior is essential to their survival. At the same time, the gerbils are learning to memorize their surroundings. Each gerbil constructs a "virtual map" in its brain, so that it knows—at any location throughout its territory—exactly how to return to its burrow in a flash.

TIP from the VETERINARIAN

Do your gerbils often gnaw at the bars of their cage? This behavior may indicate boredom. Gerbils need activity and stimulation to thrive. Provide a more interesting environment inside the cage, and give your gerbils a good variety of objects to chew on.

Standing on hind legs: Gerbils often stand tall and observe their surroundings with alert attention. The tail provides additional support and balance. Sometimes the gerbil also nods its head quickly up and down. Gerbils have an excellent sense of orientation; by observing their environment from different perspectives, they gain a three-dimensional impression of the territory.

Marking: When a male gerbil presses its belly against the ground or rubs against corners and edges, it is marking its territory. Sometime when you are holding your gerbil, turn it on its back; it's easy to identify the scent gland on its belly.

Digging: For gerbils, digging in the material that lines the cage floor is fun with a purpose. In this way, they find good nesting material and unearth food such as seeds and insects.

Eating with their paws: Like squirrels, gerbils will hold a seed in their front paws and skillfully turn it under their sharp front teeth, discarding the hull and savoring the tasty kernel.

Gnawing: Best of all, gerbils love to gnaw. Be sure to provide plenty of suitable material—it won't go to waste. After reducing branches to twigs, the gerbils will nibble the twigs to bits and the bits to shreds. Much of the material ends up as fluffy shavings in their nest.

Nest building: Building the nest calls for teamwork. When repairing or improving an existing nest, each gerbil works on its own and does what it likes. Not so when the old nest has been removed during a major cleaning. Faced with the task of building a new nest, all the adult gerbils work together, first gathering any materials that will be soft and warm. While some pack these together to form the nest, others work from the inside, burrowing and scraping and turning to create a cozy hollow.

Sleeping in the nest: Gerbils alternate between sleeping and waking, in a cycle of two to four hours. Not all the gerbils sleep at the same time. Depending on the need for warmth, the hollow of the nest may be open or closed, that is, covered over with the nest bedding.

A sisal ball offers a variety of opportunities for play. To line their sleeping nests, however, gerbils much prefer softer materials.

How Well Do You Know Your Gerbil?

You'll have more fun watching your gerbils if you understand their behavior, take good care of them, and meet their needs. Here's a little quiz to see how much you already know about your nimble little housemates. The answers are given below—but no peeking!

		YES	NO
1	Are gerbils solitary creatures?	○	○
2	Do gerbils follow a regular wake-and-sleep cycle?	○	○
3	Do gerbils have offspring only once in their lives?	○	○
4	Are nontoxic twigs good for gerbils to gnaw on?	○	○
5	Is it important for a gerbil to spend time outside its cage?	○	○
6	Do gerbils have a keen sense of smell?	○	○
7	Can gerbils live in a very small cage?	○	○
8	Is the gerbil's native habitat the dense forests of Mongolia?	○	○
9	Should a gerbil's daily diet include sunflower seeds?	○	○
10	Do gerbils enjoy sand baths?	○	○
11	Is it a good idea to pick a gerbil up by its tail?	○	○
12	Do only the mother gerbils take care of their babies?	○	○

Answers: 1 = no; 2 = yes; 3 = no; 4 = yes; 5 = yes; 6 = yes; 7 = no; 8 = no; 9 = no; 10 = yes; 11 = no; 12 = no.

Building

Claudia's three gerbils—Clickety, Clack, and Crackerjack—have learned to trust her. They will climb right onto her hand, and they even enjoy being petted. To win your gerbils' confidence, be sure that every interaction is a positive one. Otherwise, your furry friends are likely to become nervous and timid.

Trust
from the Start

love it

TIP from the THERAPIST

How quickly a gerbil becomes tame depends on its earlier experiences with humans. Try to be patient with your new pets during the adjustment period, and take care that every experience is a positive one. Otherwise your gerbils will become timid and nervous.

A Gerbil's Experience

Of course, we can't really tell for sure how gerbils are feeling, or what they are experiencing. We can't look into their minds. Based on our understanding of their natural behavior and their senses, however, we can draw some conclusions about a gerbil's feelings. Self-confident gerbils are alert, but not anxious. They search for food, build their nests, and engage in lively activity with other gerbils. Sudden and dramatic changes—for example, a new owner or a move to a strange environment—undermine this sense of security. Their first response will be to disappear into a hiding place and wait. In such stressful situations, gerbils are naturally cautious or even fearful.

However, gerbils have excellent hearing, a sensitive nose, and the ability to see what is happening all around them (see pages 21–22). They rely on their senses to provide a warning when danger threatens, but also to reassure them when all is well. Therefore, the gerbils soon adjust to the new situation and resume their lively routine. We can assume from this behavior that gerbils do feel caution, uneasiness, even fear in unusual situations, but that they can overcome these feelings and regain their sprightly aplomb.

Settling In

When you bring your gerbils home for the first time, keep in mind that they don't understand what is happening. They have left their familiar surroundings and entered an unknown environment. Ideally, your new pets already know each other and can offer mutual comfort and security. Be sure that their new home offers a ready hiding place. They'll probably dart out of sight at once, but before long their natural curiosity will win the day, and you'll see the tips of their noses and their bright eyes peering out. At last, they will venture forth to explore the unknown terrain—bit by bit, and often scooting back to the safety of their hiding place. A nest of their own helps them feel safe and secure, so you should provide straw, cardboard, and tissues that they can shred to start building their new home. It's tempting, of course, to watch and play with your new pets as much as possible. However, in their own best interest and yours as well, you should leave the gerbils in peace and quiet. Approach the cage only to replenish their food and water. As they learn their way around, they will soon feel at ease. As a rule, gerbils are so lively that they adjust to their new home within a few days. Wait for signs of curiosity that indicate your gerbils are ready to get to know you. If you rush them, it will only take longer to gain their trust.

Children and Gerbils

Gerbils make wonderful pets for children. Nimble and cute, lively and curious, they attract a child's attention and respond in kind. What's more—unlike hamsters, for instance—they are often awake and active during the daytime. Children find gerbils fascinating to watch, and their observations and discoveries about these interesting animals are remarkable. Indeed, many schools keep gerbils in the classroom as a learning opportunity. A particular benefit of keeping

Your Gerbils' Wish List

What gerbils like:

1. At least one other gerbil for company.

2. Straw, sticks and nontoxic twigs, cardboard and paper to gnaw on and shred.

3. A multilevel cage or connected cages.

4. A shallow dish full of sand to bathe in.

5. Soft material to line their nest, and plenty of bedding to dig in.

6. A weekly outing in a gerbil-proof room.

7. An undisturbed wake-and-sleep cycle of two to four hours.

8. An occasional mealworm or pumpkin seed as a tasty treat.

What gerbils don't like:

1. A boring cage with nothing to do.

2. Solitude. Gerbils need the companionship of other gerbils.

3. Being picked up by the tail, because it will break off.

4. Aggressive attention from humans.

5. Damp shavings and high humidity.

6. Excessive disturbance of their woven nest during cage cleanup.

7. Loud noise and unpleasant odors.

8. After roaming free for a time, being put back in the cage before they're ready.

gerbils, or indeed any animals, is that children learn at an early age to take responsibility for a living creature. Of course, it's important for parents to help children learn the right way to handle and care for gerbils. Children love to pick up these cute little rodents, but a gerbil has fragile bones; a fall, even a short one, could be fatal. Show your child how to hold a gerbil properly (see page 17). By the way, it's best not to locate the gerbil cage in the child's bedroom. Gerbils are active at night as well as in the daytime, and their burrowing and scuffling, not to mention a squeaky exercise wheel, might disturb the child's sleep. Also be aware that the gerbils' nighttime activities may raise dust, which the child would then inhale.

These nimble creatures need plenty of exercise and stimulation to stay fit and happy.

Tulip Tummyache

His lively curiosity has led Genghis into many a ticklish situation. Yesterday, it happened again. Ordinarily, the room where I let Genghis and Khan roam free is quite well gerbil-proofed. All the electrical cords are tucked securely away, the doors and windows are closed, houseplants are out of reach, and I move about very carefully so I won't accidentally injure my dear little companions. But this time, I forgot something—the colorful bunch of tulips that I had placed on the floor while I spread a fresh tablecloth on the table. In the few moments it took me to fetch a vase, Genghis discovered the unexpected treat and began to munch away. By the time I managed to rescue the bouquet, he had devoured two of the flowers. I was concerned, because I didn't know whether the tulips would cause him any harm. Unfortunately, not much is known about the effects of houseplants or flowers on these small creatures. Gently but quickly, I picked Genghis up. He offered no resistance as I returned him to the safety of his cage. There he stayed for the next hour or so, lying unusually still and obviously feeling less than well. Khan stood by his brother in his hour of need. Again and again, he visited Genghis and nuzzled at his head, as if to say, "You'll be better soon." Sure enough, the little patient began to recover, slowly but steadily. Apparently the only effect of his overindulgence was a tummyache, for by the next morning Genghis was bright and chipper again, ready for a new adventure.

Building Trust, Step by Step

To a gerbil, a person must look like a giant—a giant who can grab it right out of its cage and take it to strange places where all kinds of danger might lurk. What a scary feeling! At the same time, the giant brings food and water, fresh sand for bathing, sticks and twigs to gnaw on—all the things that make a gerbil happy. Little wonder that gerbils regard humans with watchful ambivalence at first. A gerbil's life depends on its alert attention to anything new and different. However, your pets won't always eye you with suspicion and dart away. Gerbils are much too curious for that! Rather, the little newcomers will soon approach you on a scouting expedition. But gerbils, somewhat like cats, have a mind of their own—don't expect them to come when you call. They will become tame, even friendly, if you make an effort to win their trust gradually, one step at a time.

It's easy to see that these two have become real pals.

Gerbils and Other Pets

Although gerbils live in harmony within their clan, and even need the companionship of other gerbils to thrive, they do not get along equally well with all other animals. Simply introducing two strange gerbils to each other calls for careful handling (see page 17). What's more, fights may break out unexpectedly even among gerbils that have been living together for quite a while. If the scuffles persist, you must intervene and separate the former comrades.

The situation can become even more problematic when animals of different species are involved. A cat, for example, sees gerbils as irresistible prey. For your pets' safety, it's best not to keep gerbils in a household with other animals.

Compatibility Test

	Young gerbil (before puberty)	Related gerbils that know each other	Unfamiliar male gerbil	Unfamiliar female gerbil	Hamster	Guinea pig	Rabbit	Rats
Young gerbil (before puberty)	♥	♥	♥	💣	💣	💣	💣	💣
Related gerbils that know each other	♥	♥	☺	☺	💣	💣	💣	💣
Unfamiliar male gerbil	♥	☺	💣	💣	💣	💣	💣	💣
Unfamiliar female gerbil	💣	☺	💣	💣	💣	💣	💣	💣
Hamster	💣	💣	💣	💣	💣	〰	💣	💣
Guinea pig	💣	💣	💣	💣	〰	♥	〰	☺
Rabbit	💣	💣	💣	💣	💣	〰	♥	💣
Rats	💣	💣	💣	💣	💣	☺	💣	♥

♥ Get along best   💣 Fur will fly   〰 Indifferent to each other   ☺ Can learn to get along

Roaming Free

A gerbil delights in the opportunity to roam free outside its cage. Finally it can scamper about to its heart's content, perhaps even playing tag or hide-and-seek with the other gerbils. Moving freely around a large area not only strengthens the gerbil's circulatory system, bones, and muscles, but also tunes its highly developed skills of orientation to its surroundings. As you can see, regular activity outside the cage keeps your gerbils fit, both physically and mentally. Be sure to offer such excursions at least once a week. Of course, these interludes also provide entertainment and a learning opportunity for you, as you watch and interact with your furry friends in this relaxed setting. When playtime is over, invite each gerbil to creep into a sturdy cardboard tube for a comfortable ride back to the cage. Another option is to set the cage on the floor with the door open, so the gerbils can return home on their own when they have tuckered themselves out.

When a gerbil has free run of the room, everything gets sniffed at, climbed on, and thoroughly explored.

A Fragrance to Forget

Every evening before dinner, I spend some time playing with my gerbils. I sit down beside them on the floor and let them climb all over me like a human jungle gym. At times like this, I'm amused to see how much Genghis and Khan differ in personality and behavior. Khan approaches me warily, one step at a time, and pauses to sniff thoroughly at my hand, but Genghis springs at me in a headlong rush. A few days ago, however, both gerbils refused to come near at all. At last, I realized why they kept their distance. I had purchased a new perfume and dabbed it on freely. Even my hands carried the scent, which I found very alluring. But Khan and Genghis thought otherwise. Quite the contrary—they were put off, because the odor masked my own personal scent, and my pets no longer recognized me. Looking startled and, I thought, even a little nauseated, they fled under the sofa. Not even my offer of a few plump sunflower seeds would entice them from their refuge. I had no choice but to take a good long shower, regretfully washing off the fragrance that I found so pleasing. Only then could I approach my two discriminating gerbils. This time, they greeted me like a long-lost pal, and the game was on.

Fun
and Games

Lively and inquisitive creatures, gerbils thrive on activity
and stimulation. They can't stand to be bored. Tame gerbils enjoy
scrambling over and playing with a familiar person, and they
love to be stroked and petted. Such interaction helps to
build a close bond between the gerbils and their
human owner.

with Gerbils

An Adventure Playground for Gerbils

If you've spent any time at all observing healthy, happy gerbils, you know that these nimble creatures are extremely alert, incredibly inquisitive, and always on the go. In order to thrive, of course, they need the companionship of other gerbils, opportunities to roam and ramble, and plenty of interesting objects to investigate and gnaw on. Be sure to offer your own gerbils a stimulating variety of safe, sturdy toys and climbing structures. Regular exercise on a playground outside the cage keeps these agile little rodents fit, and the diversity you introduce into their environment sharpens their senses.

Chewing and climbing rank as a gerbil's favorite activities. This simple wooden structure fills the bill.

What Is Your Gerbil's Personality Type?

Gerbils can have very different personalities, but they generally fall into one of two categories. Type I gerbils are lively, highly inquisitive, and very good learners. Type II gerbils tend to be more cautious; they welcome the security of a familiar daily routine. The checklist below will help you determine your gerbil's personality type.

YES   NO

1 This gerbil thoroughly investigates anything new inside the cage.

2 When allowed outside the cage, this gerbil spends most of its time in a safe hideaway.

3 This gerbil is possessive about toys and treats.

4 Even from a very low height, this gerbil doesn't dare to jump. Instead, it climbs all the way down to the ground.

5 When all the gerbils are asleep, this is the one that wakes up first, ready for new adventures.

6 This gerbil is more likely to approach and interact with the other gerbils.

7 With each litter, this mother gerbil becomes less and less vigilant.

8 This gerbil quickly grew accustomed to having your hand nearby.

9 When playing with other gerbils, this one is always more submissive.

10 Sleeping and eating are more fun for this gerbil than playing by itself for long periods of time.

Answers: If you answered "yes" to questions 1, 3, 5, 6, and 8, this gerbil has a Type I personality. If you answered "yes" to questions 2, 4, 7, 9, and 10, the gerbil has a Type II personality.

Play—A Natural Behavior

If you watch your gerbils closely as they go about their daily lives, you'll observe a wide variety of behaviors. These behaviors—some natural and instinctive, others learned or triggered by a particular situation—represent meaningful activity that would be necessary for survival in the wild. Rough-and-tumble scuffles between young gerbils train them to defend themselves against serious rivals in later life.

Digging with the paws unearths food and yields material for a cozy nest. Social grooming strengthens the bonds between group members. Even activities that look like mere play are essential to the well-being of these extremely active animals. Experience has shown that pet gerbils find plenty to do while they are on the loose—but they can't roam free all the time. Therefore, they need a spacious cage, complete with equipment that provides mental stimulation and physical activity. Consult the staff at your pet store—and use your own imagination—to create an interesting mini-playground inside your gerbils' cage. By the way, keep in mind that gerbils like to reserve certain spaces within the cage for different activities, in the same way that people use various rooms for sleeping, eating, playing, and so on. Therefore, one way to add interest and variety is to choose a multilevel cage or, if space permits, to connect two or three cages with tunnels to create a larger living complex.

On this mini-playground, the gerbils can demonstrate all their skills.

How Happy Is Your Gerbil?

What sorts of things do you give your gerbils to gnaw on?

- None
  0 points
- Hay or straw
  1 point
- Wood, paper, cardboard
  2 points

How often do you let your gerbils roam free outside their cage?

- Never
  0 points
- Once a month
  1 point
- At least once a week
  2 points

Do you give your gerbils lots of sunflower seeds in their daily diet?

- Yes
  0 points
- No
  1 point

How many playmates does your gerbil have?

- None
  0 points
- One
  2 points
- Several
  2 points

What does your pet's fur look like?

- Thick, glossy
  1 point
- Straggly, matted, damp
  0 points

How often do you provide animal protein (such as mealworms)?

- Never
  0 points
- Occasionally
  1 point
- Often
  0 points

Do your gerbils have the opportunity to take sand baths?

- Yes
  1 point
- No
  0 points

Is the cage located in a dry, warm, bright place?

- Yes
  1 point
- No
  0 points

How often do you clean the cage?

- Once a week
  2 points
- Once a month
  1 point
- Four times a year
  0 points

Do you observe your gerbils' behavior to learn more about them?

- Sometimes
  0 points
- Every day
  1 point
- No
  0 points

0–5 points: You should be seriously concerned about your gerbils' well-being. **6–11 points:** You are taking good care of your pets. Keep it up! Try to learn more about what your gerbils need; they will do even better in the future. **12–14 points:** Congratulations! Your gerbils are fortunate to have an owner who cares so much about them.

Knock, Knock!

Understanding how gerbils communicate can prove very useful. When a gerbil is alarmed and senses danger, it will drum its hind legs on the ground to warn the other gerbils in its clan. I've taken advantage of this to keep my small friends in line. Both Genghis and Khan find my wool carpet enormously attractive. The minute I take my eye off them, they nibble away at its braided edge. Apparently the wool is of very high quality—just what they need for the soft lining of their nest. The gerbils don't care one whit that this doesn't meet with my approval. To save the carpet, I needed to come up with a trick. One day, I had an inspiration. First, I practiced drumming my fingers in the same rhythm that my gerbils use to signal each other when danger threatens. The next time Genghis and Khan started their campaign of destruction, I sounded the alarm. At once, the little rodents stopped their work, raised their heads, and sniffed the air for signs of danger. Just then, a happy accident rein-forced my warning message. The hard-boiled egg that lay beside my plate rolled off the table and landed with a dull thud right behind Genghis and Khan. Quick as a wink, the two startled nibblers scurried away to the safety of their cage.

Excellent Adventures

Of course, you'll want to make your gerbils' time outside the cage an adventure. Ordinary household objects provide entertainment at no extra cost. The gerbils will happily nibble on a crust of stale bread, apple peels or cores, or a leaf of lettuce, and they'll rummage eagerly through a pile of nutshells in search of edible remnants. They'll crawl through all sorts of cardboard tubes, then shred them to bits; clean egg cartons are also great to gnaw on. You might crumple a handful of paper towels and toss it on the floor, or cut holes in a cardboard shoe box to improvise a cave. Your gerbils will soon let you know which activities suit them best.

Pet stores, too, offer a wide assortment of toys for gerbils—from wooden towers and tunnels to swings and nests woven of sisal cord, all just the right size for your little pets.

TIP from the PET STORE

There's nothing gerbils like better than to nibble and gnaw. Therefore, when you choose toys for your gerbils, look for items made of wood (such as wooden ladders and towers) instead of plastic. Swallowed pieces of plastic can be hazardous to a gerbil's health.

This climbing structure swivels to challenge the gerbil's highly developed sense of orientation.

Active and Happy

Speedy, the gerbil on the right, is already three years old; little Tito was born just six weeks ago. The old-timer and the youngster get along very well, even though Speedy can't keep up with Tito when they scamper around the room. Tito treats the older gerbil with the respect he deserves as a senior member of the clan.

in Old Age

old & happy

How Long Do Gerbils Live?

Scientists have studied Mongolian gerbils in their native habitat to determine how long they live. In the wild, these small rodents survive for no more than about six months. Little wonder, for they have many natural enemies. In particular, polecats and owls prey on gerbils. Pet gerbils, given proper care, live three to four times as long as their wild counterparts. The reasons are obvious: They are safe from pre-dators, and their diet—in contrast to conditions in the wild—is abundant,

balanced, and varied. Biologists take the view that the primary purpose of all living creatures, whether plants or animals, is to propagate their species, that is, to reproduce. Although one might still ask how the individual gerbil can be said to benefit from this endeavor, the fact remains that with a total of some 25 to 60 immediate offspring in the wild (and easily twice that many in captivity), the gerbil has clearly done its duty. Biological theories notwithstanding, gerbil fanciers judge by other standards. They value not the reproductive

The Autumn of Life

➡ **Appearance:**
With age, a gerbil's coat may show a few gray hairs here and there.

➡ **Behavior:**
Gerbils enjoy the same activities in old age as in their younger days, though they usually become a bit less frisky and more cautious in their adventures.

➡ **Social Interactions:**
Older gerbils are less inclined to romp around with others, and not as quick to get involved in a scrap. Younger gerbils treat the senior members of the group with considerably greater respect.

➡ **Diet:**
Older gerbils need less protein than younger ones. Seeds with a high fat content, such as sunflower seeds, can cause health problems if given too frequently. Watch an older gerbil's weight, and be sure to provide plenty of exercise outside the cage.

➡ **Hearing:**
The ability to hear high tones diminishes. An older gerbil now hears deeper tones best.

➡ **Health:**
The risk of tumors increases. Cardiovascular problems (such as strokes) are more common, especially if the diet is high in fat.

efficiency of gerbils as a species, but the pleasure of interacting with each individual little gerbil—a pleasure that endures for every day of the gerbil's long and happy life.

How Gerbils Die

The two most common causes of death for gerbils are diseases and age-related ailments, most commonly involving tumors.

Diseases often result from improper care. Perhaps the diet is not balanced, or the cage is exposed to drafts. Perhaps the gerbils are too crowded and fight among themselves, or they lack adequate material to gnaw on. Such stressful situations weaken the animals' immune system. Without appropriate intervention, the gerbils are vulnerable to illnesses that can end in death. Concrete examples include

➜ Severe colds and respiratory ailments (typically resulting from exposure to a damp or chilly environment).

➜ Prolonged diarrhea (caused by an improper diet or spoiled food, infections, and internal parasites).

➜ Seizures (earlier strains were particularly susceptible to epilepsy. The problem is increasingly less common).

Even though older gerbils are less spry than before, they still enjoy playing, exploring, and nibbling on a healthy snack.

TIP from the VETERINARIAN

A layperson has no way of knowing how much a sick gerbil is suffering. If your gerbil shows signs of illness, you should consult a veterinarian right away. The veterinarian will determine whether the ailment can be cured or the gerbil should be euthanized.

If you observe your gerbils regularly, you may notice the warning signs of health problems. The sick animal isolates itself from the group, loses weight, has a matted coat, seems less agile, huddles listlessly in a corner of the cage, or even falls onto its side before death finally ends its misery. In such situations, consult a veterinarian (see *Tip*, above). If the disease is infectious, you should take steps to protect the other gerbils.

One cause of death in baby gerbils is particularly gruesome: They are eaten by their own mother. This can happen for various reasons. One may be that the mother suddenly feels an irresistible craving for protein. To prevent this, be sure to give the mother a high-protein diet while she is pregnant and nursing her young. Cannibalism may also occur if the mother gerbil and her babies don't get the peace and quiet they need. This causes the mother severe stress.

Even a gerbil that manages to stay healthy will eventually die, of course. This usually happens after about three years (in very rare cases, up to five years). A gerbil that dies of old age generally goes quietly. One day, you will simply find its dead body in the cage.

Saying Good-bye

Whether a gerbil dies of illness or old age, parting can be difficult. Our small companions—so sprightly, so engaging—have found their way into our hearts, and we miss them when they die. The sight of the lifeless little body arouses a flood of memories of the nimble creature darting about the cage in happier days. Tending to the solitary gerbil or the smaller group that remains, we feel a keen sense of loss.

Adults recognize the end of a gerbil's life as a natural occurrence, but children, especially if this is their first encounter with death, need support from adults. Listen to their feelings, and let them cry. It might help to bring out photos or videotapes of their beloved pet, or share memories of its familiar ways and amusing antics.

Finally, you might help them to bury the gerbil's body in your own yard or garden, or in a nearby grove or meadow. The ceremony offers an opportunity to express and acknowledge sadness, and you can remember the departed companion together when you pass by or visit the grave.

When a Gerbil Loses Its Partner

Just as you and your family miss a gerbil after its death, in all likelihood the gerbil's surviving mate feels the loss keenly as well. Of course, we don't know for sure how gerbils experience the death of another gerbil. However, gerbils are essentially monogamous, so it's natural to assume that the remaining gerbil misses its mate. Likewise, when a pair of gerbils of the same sex have shared a cage, the survivor will probably be lonely after its familiar companion dies. Now it has no sparring partner, no comrade for mutual grooming and cuddling. On the other hand, if several gerbils have lived together, the death of one member of the group is less severely felt. Keep this in mind when separating a large group of gerbils into several cages (see page 18).

If you are left with one surviving gerbil, you should take steps to give it the companionship it needs. Keep in mind, however, that if you introduce a young gerbil as a companion to a single much older gerbil, you will most likely face the same situation again soon. A better solution is to add a pair of younger gerbils. When the older one eventually dies, the two that remain will have approximately the same life expectancy. Introducing new gerbils to the older survivor can present problems (see page 17), as can integrating a single gerbil into an existing group. However, it's not impossible. The key to success is patience. If for some reason you are unable to add one or more new gerbils, all is not lost. Be sure to give the solitary gerbil extra attention. Supply an ample variety of objects to chew on, along with

Keeping a group of gerbils that are the same age has advantages. If one gerbil dies, the others still have the companionship they need.

plenty of nesting material. Both inside the cage and during regular excursions, provide as much entertainment, exercise, and stimulation as possible.

When One Gerbil of a Clan Dies

When a gerbil loses its mate or its only companion, it will be lonely, at least for a while. When one gerbil of a larger group dies, loneliness is not an issue, but the death can have an effect on the social structure of the clan. To the outside observer, it appears that the loss of a gerbil is not particularly distressful to the remaining group if the departed gerbil is of relatively low rank. By contrast, the sudden absence of an older gerbil that has held a

position of leadership within the clan usually has serious consequences. The older, dominant gerbils—as long as they can maintain their rank—are the authorities that all the others respect. For example, you may see one of them intervene when two younger gerbils are fighting. The two belligerents defer to the leader, and peace returns to the cage.

Therefore, the death of one of these leaders, whether male or female, does not go unnoticed. Rather, the next-ranking tier of gerbils begins to jostle for dominance. The resulting skirmishes may be fierce at times, but eventually the group will recognize a new leader. You need not intervene unless the battles get out of hand.

Yogurt and mealworms are good sources of protein. Keep in mind that older gerbils need less protein than youngsters that are still growing.

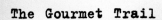

The Gourmet Trail

One of the activities Genghis and Khan enjoy most is following a food trail. Every now and then, while they are playing outside their cage, I set out morsels of their favorite foods—raisins, pumpkin seeds, nuts, and a few sunflower seeds—in a line around the room. Following their dainty noses, Genghis and Khan gobble up one tasty tidbit after another. With a food trail, I can lead the eager fellows just about anywhere. A few days ago, I even tried ending the trail back in their enclosure. The last morsel lay on the ramp formed by the open cage door. But my gerbils were more clever than I had thought. They knew exactly what was going on. If they followed the trail all the way into their cage, their time of freedom would come to an end—and neither Genghis nor Khan was ready for that. So, to my astonishment, the little scamps simply left the last raisin on the door and went back to their adventures. I didn't have the heart to return them to their cage, for it was clear that they had not had enough of the exercise that every gerbil needs. Two more hours passed before they grew tired and sought out their sleeping nest, this time without any trickery on my part. Curled up side by side, they fell sound asleep, no doubt to dream of a never-ending trail of gourmet delights.

Index

Engelbert Kötter
has kept and bred gerbils for many years. He ranks as a pioneer in the field of species-appropriate care of gerbils. His two books about gerbils, published in German by Gräfe und Unzer, did much to increase the popularity of gerbils as household pets.

Christine Steimer
is a dedicated animal photographer. She works for international book publishers, specialized journals, and advertising agencies.

Gabriele Linke-Grün
has worked for many years as a freelance writer for the Gräfe und Unzer nature book series and for various animal magazines and textbook publishers. She wrote the *Gerbil Adventures*.

The moss would make a soft bed—but who's sleepy?

Books

Kötter, Engelbert. *Gerbils.* Hauppauge, NY: Barron's Educational Series, Inc., 1999.

Petty, Kate. *First Pets: Gerbils.* Hauppauge, NY: Barron's Educational Series, Inc., 1995.

Piers, Helen. *Taking Care of Your Gerbils*. Hauppauge, NY: Barron's Educational Series, Inc., 1993.

Putnam, Perry. *Guide to Owning a Gerbil.* Neptune, NJ: TFH Publications, 1997.

Organizations

American Veterinary Medical Association
1931 North Meachem Road
Suite 100
Schaumburg, IL 60173-4360
(847) 925-8070
http://www.avma.org

American Society of Mammalogists
H. Duane Smith, Secretary-Treasurer
Monte L. Bean Life Sciences Museum
Brigham Young University
Provo, UT 84602-0200
http://asm.wku.edu

Acknowledgments

The photographer and the publisher wish to thank the firm Wagner & Keller of Ludwigshafen, Germany, for its gracious support. The company has worked successfully for many years to promote suitable conditions in bird and animal shelters.

English translation
© Copyright 2002 by
Barron's Educational Series, Inc.

Original title of the book
in German is
Meine Rennmaus und ích
Copyright © 2000 by Gräfe und
Unzer Verlag GmbH, Munich

English translation by
Celia Bohannon

All inquiries should be addressed to:
Barron's Educational Series, Inc.
250 Wireless Boulevard
Hauppauge, NY 11788
http://www.barronseduc.com

International Standard Book No. 0-7641-1923-0

Library of Congress Catalog Card
No. 00-112035

Printed in Hong Kong

9 8 7 6 5 4 3 2 1

These Are My Gerbils

If you go away on vacation, or if you are sick, a friend or neighbor might have to take care of your pets for a while. In the spaces below, you can write helpful notes about your gerbils.

My gerbils' names:

1

2

The color of their fur:

1

2

How I recognize my gerbils:

1

2

What I feed my gerbils:

Favorite special treats:

Tips for handling my gerbils:

How to take care of my gerbils: